real & raw

K.S. Elliott

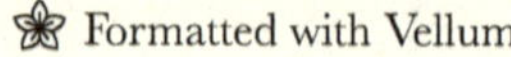 Formatted with Vellum

for myself

real & raw isn't a poetry collection full of pretty prose, heartbreaking and haunting words. It is as the title says: real & raw.

It ventures into the depths of my soul, my mind, the things I have felt in the past, still feel in the present, and my fears for the future.

This will not be easy to read, my mind is not full of pixie dust and sunshine as some may think.

So please, I beg of you, read responsibly.

Mentions of:

— suicide
— suicidal thoughts
— self harm
— death
— grief
— psychosis
— anxiety
— depression
— drugs
— alcohol
— self hatred
— loss of a baby
— rape
— domestic violence

Now, after reading this, I hope you understand the gravity of what I'm telling you. Here and in the acknowledgements, there will be a list of organisations that you can call if you need it. These are only the Australian numbers, but no matter where you are in the world, there is a number that you can call.

Lifeline: 13 11 14

Beyond Blue: 1300 224 636
For Aboriginal and Torres Strait Islanders, 13YARN
provides free and confidential crisis support.

It's dark in the following pages,
please read at your own discretion.

Welcome to the darkest reaches of my mind.

whenever i'm alone
i tend to fall
deep into the darkness that is my mind
i'm never alone
but when i am...
god only knows what goes on in the darkness
it is not kind by any means
it is cruel
it is torture
it is dark
so very dark
i haven't torn my skin apart in years
but whenever i am alone
it plagues my mind
how would it feel now that i am grown?
would it hurt less?
more?
would i go deeper than i dared as a child?
or am i too scared?
god i'm scared
i voice my thoughts
fears
anxieties
and hopes
more than anyone i've ever known
but this darkness?
that is mine and mine alone
i couldn't express the lack of light if i tried
there's no light at the end of the tunnel
i'm not even sure it is a tunnel
it is too dark
too deep
i may never make it out

it hurts too much
i'm too tired
i want to embrace the darkness
become what it whispers me to
i want to become one with this darkness of mine

heads cloudy, thoughts racing
spiralling down a rabbit of
am i good enough?
do i have to wake up tomorrow?
i could smoke a blunt, even though i haven't in months
my time is borrowed
can i give it back?
life is too long
and i'm too tired to keep moving forward
oh these sunday blues

no matter how much i voice
what's on my mind
it screams to tell someone
anyone
just how broken and bruised i am
how it torments me
with my worst qualities
and greatest fears
i have never been able to explain
just how opposite i feel
i understand now that the expression is:
ineffable
it is ineffable to me that i feel
so lonely
yet i'm surrounded by people
it is ineffable to me that i feel
complete
yet so incomplete
it's torture
everything i feel has it's opposite
and i feel that too
i'm a mirror of every cursed feeling

resilience is a curse
do not envy those
with the strength to continue
when all else crumbles around them
for they would like nothing more
than to collapse into the rubble
never to stand again
resilience is a curse
we do not get to our feet
because we feel we have to
we pick ourselves up
because what other choice do we have?
it is either
continue
even when we desperately don't want to
or
reach into the chests
of everyone we've ever loved
snatch their hearts
forever broken
now what kind of person
would that make us?
it is simple ethics
them or me?
and so
that is why you should not envy
those with resilience
because we don't truly want to stand again

the mind is so complex
don't you think?
how can i be so happy
yet want to scream?
how i can't express anger
yet want to break
everything and anything
but mostly myself
open my brain so maybe
i could finally understand
the inexplicable feelings i feel
the paralysing hate of myself
and this world
the constant agony flipped
off and on like a switch
i think about you sometimes
i want to ask you
what flicked that switch?
what was the final straw?
how do you know when enough is enough?
and finally
where did the courage come from to jump?

woven in the trauma of your past
turning that hurt into something that will last
a web of deceit that you honestly believe
there was never enough of you for me
i don't hate you
but i do blame you
you chose this
you chose me
though you didn't want me
not truly
i know you love me
you support me
you want me to be free
but how can i be free when i'm held inside a cage

i feel like i'm going into a psychosis
i've never experienced it before but this is how i imagine it
would feel like
my mind never shuts off
never
even in the late hours of the night
i have a constant ticking in my head
a clock counting down the minutes
until i can't anymore
can't breathe
can't speak
can't live

i'm not suicidal but don't ask me if i'm okay
the answer is so simple
yet so far away

i am a bushfire but a tsunami
a beautiful yet chaotic waltz
that's what it's like inside my head
it doesn't make sense
nothing fits
no matter the thought or idea
i always have opposing opinions
trust me, i know
it's hard in here, i'm aware
i can't go one minute without weighing the options
i'm scared of the world
i'm scared of birds and bugs
they're just like me
wandering the world with no plans
no destination
no destiny

it's hard up in here
always saying yes but always saying no
atlantis on repeat

i'm screaming now
in my car where no one can hear me
but i'm screaming
i haven't screamed for death to come and take me in a long time
he may even hear me this time around
come to my door
take me from this place.
i would like to go with death, i think
he seems kind behind the exterior
lost, even

"death is my friend"

"did she just say death?"
my mother gasped because she knew
death only came out to play when i was in a psychosis

i want to turn it off
i can't deal
does that make me too soft?
i want to turn it all off
waiting for a car to swerve
so that i can get what i deserve
more so what i desire
sit me on top of a funeral pyre
i want to meet my maker
maybe they'll have the answer

tell me why the world would break her
take her
make her
into someone who's a forsaker
i can't keep screaming in my car
i can't keep creating scars
i just want to be among the stars
maybe there i'll be a rockstar

i can't control this anger inside of me
it's inside of me and it's festering
it's festering deep into my bones
my bones filled with anger
need to atone
need to atone
but for what?
the doors to my heart closed shut
nothing could pry them open again
blood on my thighs, when then?

when i first started feeling like i couldn't breathe
i didn't know this thing was inside of me
it was
black smoke
pure evil burrowing deep
seeped into my bones
shit felt like ecstasy

i want to burn this place into the ground
everything's always hurting
i don't know where this anger came from
i don't know why i need to scream
on an uphill but i can't stop going down

help me
i can't stop bleeding
find me—
not her
the real me

fading in and out
i've lost my mind
this evil and i are intertwined
everything replaced by anger
please tell me you'll be my anchor
i can't control this darkness
it hurts too much
i'm too tired
i want to embrace the dark
become what it whispers me to

i want to become one
with this darkness of mine
but if i look devoid
of emotion
the first thing you should do is run
at least i know i've had enough
this anger has only just begun

pulling myself apart
almost crashed my car
numb from all the smoke
tearing at my skin
empty vessel i am in

heart on my sleeve
but it's just a tattoo
you created the ruin
the devil is dancing under my skin
he said it's time for the execution

forgiveness is a curse
a nicety we all must rehearse
why should i forgive?
why must i confess?
what sins could i have
that you did not cause?
walls that you made
surround my mind
but the me that's behind
she's screaming for help

being with me is not easy
i will replay the words that leave your lips
i will become paranoid
you're going to rip my heart from my chest
leave me behind
but i promise i'm not crazy
well maybe
i will sit on god's doorstep
ask her to forgive my sins
promise her i will never sin again
if it meant i got to lie with you
not make love
just lie there
listening to your heart
while you rub sleepy circles on my back
i will fight for my life to have you in it
i will throw sticks and stones
i will break bones
see…
i promised god i wouldn't sin again
if i could keep you
but if i had to sin
to keep you
i would make nice with the devil
dance his dance
hand in hand
i promise i'm not crazy
but for you?
i'll break everything inside of me
just to hold you together

it is odd to think that my life has actually happened
to know that it is not a tale or tragically made movie
it happened
it all…
happened
maybe it is best to believe it was a tale
than to know it as a reality

the world has told me that i am too much for too long
so when i ask you if i am too much
do not simply say no
tell me that my loudness is the only thing you yearn to hear
tell me that my eyes are all you yearn to see
my skin is all that you yearn to touch
and my perfume is all that you yearn to smell
tell me that i am not too much
tell me that what they perceived as too much
was, in fact, more than enough

"grief will become easier with time" my mother said
why would i want this grief to subside?
at every memory
every tug of my heart
every lump in my throat
and every tear that i shed
is the love that i have
but cannot express

mirror mirror on the wall
why is my figure distorted?
my smile could light up a room
pull all of my teeth out
my skin is glowing
cover it up
eyes are golden in the sun
when will the moon rise again?
compliments on the tattoos etched into my skin
cut them out
cut them out
cut them out

mirror mirror
why do i keep on looking
if you aren't kind to me?
i can't help it
feed my insecurities

i feel like i'm relapsing
i feel like i'm fourteen again
i haven't felt like this in a while
not to this extent
thoughts of sin
i must repent
suicidal thoughts slipping back in to torment me
maybe this time i'll bring myself to wrap my car around a tree

why am i like this?
why do i hate myself?
but i don't hate myself
i'm a walking fucking contradiction
i'm so sick of myself
yet i'm so happy with who i am
i don't want to live inside my head anymore
they're my family
so why the fuck am i procrastinating going inside?
just get out of the fucking car
go inside
you're pathetic

why sit up with me until early hours of morning
voicing our opinions on the world
and you seeing tears in my eyes
because i opened up to you about how i am
unable to escape my own mind?
why sit up with me until early hours of morning
telling me you're sorry i got broken
if you were just going to add to that broken heart?
why does other's judgement matter
when the only judgement that matters is our own?
we got along so well
i thought you'd be my maid of honour
that would make you laugh
why allow me to give you a key to open my heart
and mind
and soul
if you were just going to confuse my mind
mark my soul
and break my heart?

my anxiety is chewing through my veins
soon anxiety will be all that remains
my corpse rotting six feet under
i'm sorry but all i can do is wonder
when you die you find peace, right?
so why can't i go tonight?

i wonder what you would've looked like
what colour your eyes would have been
i wonder what we would have fought about
how much trouble we'd get in
i'd pick you up after every heartbreak
and put you back together again

i would have taught you how to walk and talk
when you got older we would talk about girls
i would have taught you all the ways of the world
i would have kept all your secrets safe
i would have helped you every step of the way
but these are just what if's and my imagination
because you're not here to tell the story
of how your life would have gone

our lives are different worlds
you are always busy, care free
i'm at home thinking why me?
why would you choose the girl who picks at her fingernails?
the girl who has to wear a jumper otherwise she feels
exposed
why would you choose the girl who thinks that she is
worthless?
can't go one minute without forcing tears back
why wouldn't you choose a blonde with a hourglass body
who's carefree?
why wouldn't you choose a blonde who loves going out
with her friends?
why wouldn't you choose a blonde who's independent?
she doesn't irritate you by being at your side
every second
and gets upset when she isn't
why wouldn't you choose anyone other than me?
me who notices you staring at other girls
but won't get mad at you for it
me who gets scared to go out
because people will stare
talk about it
me who will cry at the smallest inconvenience
me who is scared that i'm not going to amount to anything
me who has a fucked up mind
why me and not a blonde?

maybe lately i've just given up on people
i give out my heart
then they turn out to be evil
making my heart break
making me feeble
lately i think i've just given up on people

i guess the consequence of my happiness is to heighten my anxiety
all this self doubt is going to kill me quietly
when i try to talk it's choking up inside of me
fuck
i'm a disappointment
and i'm wearing my heart on my sleeve
i'm used to watching people leave
so don't worry about me
i'll be fine if you go
though i've been thinking of letting myself go
this place is too cruel for my heart
i'm too weak
and it's too dark
let me go
i want to be with the stars
let me go
i want to see what it's like on mars

i've been imprisoned in my mind
it's eating me alive
i don't know how much more i can take
i can't escape
i want to be rid of this world
where we need to be in 'good shape'
and where young girls get raped
god someone please help

i'm hurting more than i show
i'm broken in ways you wouldn't know
my heart beats
but i'm not alive
i look fine
but i'm more than dead inside
you can see that i'm broken
look into my eyes
can't you tell that this smile is my disguise?

i just can't take this pain anymore
i'm sorry
the pieces of my heart are scattered across the floor
all of the times i told you i'm just tired
i wasn't wanting to dream
that was me letting out an almost silent scream

i will never be able to escape this jail cell
this one inside my head
pessimistic messages written along the walls
the floor
and ceiling
telling me i should be dead

do i really crave love that much
to a point where i let you manipulate me?
we both knew what you were doing
yet i let it be
i must be crazy
how did we not know
that we were a catastrophe in the making?
love made me blind—
no
you manipulated my mind
told me pretty lies in the dark
when the sun came up
you'd made your mark
i had no hope of escaping

humanity has normalised depression
drugs
and alcohol
i was in the mix
so i didn't stand out to anyone at all
now that i'm succeeding
with all of that in the past
i can't even whisper
without the world hearing how much i've surpassed

i don't need to force someone to fit
if they are meant to be
they will fit with ease
they are the ones who make you want to be better
because you've noticed they light up your world when they are near
when someone does not bring you that joy
they simply do not fit
i should have never forced someone to fit
when you were the piece that i was missing

why can't this darkness inside me cease to exist?
i try to be optimistic
but it continues to persist
everything in black and white
i know how to succeed
but there's no light
i'm missing out on pink, green, and sky blues
i'm missing out on all kinds of beautiful views
with my mind as dull as an overcast, moonless night
with you by my side
i feel almost fine
i want to see the sun
and because of you
one day i just might

will you wait for me?
while i unlearn all of the things
that i was taught
all of the lies
that were spun
will you wait for me?
as i figure out my truth
as i learn who i am
will you wait for me?

"pressure makes diamonds"
but that's not true
sometimes, when the pressure is too heavy, too much
it can sink you entirely
drown you
and you may have put those weights on your shoulders
yourself
pushed yourself to carry a weight that you cannot hold
but remember: you are allowed to take those weights off
allow yourself to float back up to the surface
become an emerald instead
because let's be honest
emeralds are prettier than diamonds anyway

someone once asked me who i am
i told them my name
"no, who are you?"
it took me a moment
but then i realised
i'm someone who feels so deeply it hurts
someone who used to sit in a tree with her person
and play make believe
because our imaginations ran wild
mine still do
even though you're not here
i use my imagination to have you by my side
i'm someone who wants to feel alive
see everything the world has to offer
love with everything inside of me
and to be loved with that same fire back
i want to feel the sand between my toes
and know that as long as i am truthful to myself
that i will know who i am

acknowledgements

You doing okay? If not, I'd like to remind you that there are amazing organisations across the world that can help you. Below, I will list the Australian numbers, but no matter where you are in the world, there are alternate numbers you can call.

Lifeline: 13 11 14
Beyond Blue: 1300 224 636
For Aboriginal and Torres Strait Islanders, 13YARN
provides free and confidential crisis support.

real & raw was never meant to be something.

My poems were never meant to see the light of day, only told to those who've heard them before at 2 a.m. when I'm intoxicated—but here we are. And there are multiple people who I'd like to thank for pushing me to put my deepest, darkest thoughts out there; however, there is one person in particular who made this happen.

Let me set the scene.

I had too much on my plate, way too much for any one person—which is where the "pressure makes diamonds" poem came from—and a reader of mine, a friend, really, commented on one of my videos and told me she needed a poetry book from me. I dismissed it, always have when someone said that, but that night…I broke. I realised I couldn't handle all of the weight I put on my shoulders and decided to take some of the weight off. It was a hard choice to make, but it was the right one. I then wrote the "pressure makes diamonds" poem and suddenly it clicked. I have always promised to be real, to be raw, it's what has shaped me, made me, created the person that I am today.

And thus, real & raw was born.

And it's all thanks to Danielle.

So thank you. Even though you didn't know what you set in motion when you said it, I will eternally be grateful for that push. For your belief in me.

I'd also, as always, love to thank my beautiful cover designer, Ebony (@ebonyjadetattoos) When I messaged you outside of work hours asking if you'd be up for another project, you didn't hesitate. You asked me what I was thinking, I brain dumped everything onto you, and you said yes instantly. You said you would be honoured to create this cover, and though it isn't extravagant, I can assure everyone that Ebony put thought into every little thing. You are amazing, and I am so grateful that I know you.

Thank you to everyone who hurt me. Who ripped my heart from my chest, threw it to the floor, and stomped on it for good measure. You taught me many things, but you also gave me something to write about. And for that I'll forever be grateful.

And lastly, of course, thank you to YOU. You who is reading this. I am truly sorry if my words made you hurt, made you cry, but I just wanted to let you know that you are not alone. You have never been alone. When I wrote a lot of these poems, I thought that I was alone. That no one could wholly understand my mind and heart, and honestly, I still feel that way. But it is with a heart so full of hope that even one person who reads this can understand. Relate. And not because I want you to hurt. Never that. But because then, I—and you—will finally know that we are not alone.

about the author

K.S. Elliott, when not writing or coming up with another million ideas, is usually holed up with a good book, her cat, Marcia, cuddled up with her. On the weekends you can usually find her with the people she loves, at the beach, or finding something new to do.

If you'd like to get into contact with K.S. Elliott or simply follow her socials, here they are!

https://ks-elliott.myshopify.com

also by K.S. Elliott

Redemption of Omnia duology

Both available on Amazon, Kindle Unlimited, or on the author's website for signed copies

https://ks-elliott.myshopify.com

www.ingramcontent.com/pod-product-compliance
Lightning Source LLC
LaVergne TN
LVHW051021080826
845145LV00009B/2735

* 9 7 8 1 7 6 4 1 6 8 2 4 3 *